Life in the Bluegrass
A Pictorial History 1940-1970

PRESENTED BY THE LEXINGTON HERALD-LEADER

ACKNOWLEDGMENTS

Many thanks to the citizens of Central Kentucky, whose sharing of their family photographs made this book possible.

The text was written by *Herald-Leader* staff writer Andy Mead.

Other photographs in this book were graciously provided by these organizations:

Georgetown and Scott County Museum

Jessamine County Historical Society

Lexington History Museum

Lexington Safety Museum

Transylvania University Library

University of Kentucky Libraries

John C. Wyatt Lexington Herald-Leader Collection

Woodford County Historical Society Museum

Copyright© 2007   •   ISBN: 1-59725-112-7

Published by Pediment Publishing, a division of The Pediment Group, Inc. www.pediment.com Printed in Canada

TABLE OF CONTENTS

FOREWORD

In the early 1940s, when the earliest photos in this book were taken, Lexington was a sleepy little Southern town. By 1970, it was a whole 'nother place.

In three decades the city got a modern airport and a large new industrial and manufacturing base. And it attracted people. The population of Fayette County hit 100,000 in 1950, 132,000 in 1960 and 174,000 in 1970, making it one of the fastest-growing cities in the nation.

Along the way, it became the retail, service and social heart for a large part of Kentucky.

Some of that expansion and maturation shows in the photos of this book. But what shows most are the people who lived through that surge. Maybe your grandparents or parents. You might even find yourself in here.

COMMERCE

The business culture of the Bluegrass is continually evolving. The changes came at an increasingly rapid rate in the 1940s, '50s and '60s, preparing us for what has become the norm today.

In the beginning of the period, one could still find men sitting around a country store, just as their fathers had done a century before. World War II brought women into the workforce, and by the mid-1950s, men and women were working side-by-side on an assembly line, putting together typewriters for a new company in town — IBM.

Just outside of town, horses and mules were giving way to great, awkward pieces of machinery that turned earth and harvested crops.

Some venerable old buildings disappeared in the name of progress. The Ben Ali theater on Main Street was razed. A block along West Broadway bit the dust, later to be reincarnated at Triangle Park. But the elaborate cast-iron façade of the Melodian survived and still graces Main Street at Upper. And those who take a few minutes to drive out to Russell Cave and Iron Works pikes can still get a sandwich at the Jot 'Em Down Store.

Typewriter assembly at the IBM plant, circa 1956. The July 1, 1956, Sunday edition of the *Lexington Herald-Leader* formally announced the impending arrival of a new IBM factory for its electric typewriter division. The new industry was welcomed for its outstanding employee and community relations. *Courtesy of Lexington History Museum*

Grand opening of the new location of Fitzgerald Drugs, 229 W. Main St., Frankfort, May 1941. *Courtesy of Tom Fitzgerald*

Kroger store, Main Street, Versailles, 1942. *Courtesy of David Dearinger*

Construction of the Lexington Signal Depot, 1941. *Courtesy of University of Kentucky Libraries 1.13-318.03*

Employees of the Irving parachute factory on Versailles Road, circa 1942. Lelia Farris is on the left in the back row. *Courtesy of Mary Jo Smith*

Curry's Drug Store in the Central Exchange Bank building at the corner of Short and Upper streets, March 1946. *Courtesy of University of Kentucky Libraries 1.13-129*

Paint Lick Ferry ran between Jessamine and Garrard counties. Mike Hurt operated the ferry by pulling the cable by hand, July 17, 1943. *Courtesy of Howard C. Teater*

Melodian Hall on the southeast corner of Main and Upper streets, Lexington, 1941. *Courtesy of Transylvania University Library, J. Winston Coleman Jr. Collection*

Tobacco auction sales in Fayette County, December 1942. *Courtesy of Transylvania University Library, J. Winston Coleman Jr. Collection*

View of the west side of South Broadway between Main and Water streets, Lexington, June 1943. Lexington Roller Mills, the five-story building in the distance, was razed in July 1970. *Courtesy of Transylvania University Library, J. Winston Coleman Jr. Collection*

Jot 'Em Down Store, Fayette County, July 1943. The business was located at the southwest corner of the Russell Cave and Iron Works pikes. Lucien Terrell, whose children are in front of the store, operated the business and lived with his family on the second floor. *Courtesy of Transylvania University Library, J. Winston Coleman Jr. Collection*

M.S. Rawlins Country Store at Donerail, Fayette County, 1943. *Courtesy of Transylvania University Library, J. Winston Coleman Jr. Collection*

M.S. Rawlins Country Store at Donerail, Fayette County, 1943. *Courtesy of Transylvania University Library, J. Winston Coleman Jr. Collection*

Aerial view of Cheapside, 1943. *Courtesy of Transylvania University Library, J. Winston Coleman Jr. Collection*

Texaco service station at the corner of Colfax and Limestone streets, circa 1944. During the World War II years, patrons would need ration coupons to purchase gas. The owner, Raymond Freeman, then turned those coupons in to receive his gas allotment for the next fill from his supplier. *Courtesy of Linda Freeman White*

View along Water Street looking west, Lexington, 1944. Included are Samuel D. McCullough's mustard factory, the police station and the Lexington and Ohio Railroad depot. The buildings were razed circa 1961. *Courtesy of Transylvania University Library, J. Winston Coleman Jr. Collection*

Betty Boyd enjoying a Coke in her father's store, Reynolds Grocery on Virginia Avenue, 1945. A.B. Reynolds operated the store. *Courtesy of Betty Boyd*

Stripping bluegrass seed, June 1946. *Courtesy of Lexington History Museum*

Packaging Starks' Headache Powder for distribution, April 1949. The business was founded by Richard Starks in 1873 and later operated by his daughter, Edna Hicks, for 35 years. The powder was made, packaged and shipped from Midway to places all over the world. From left to right: Martha Clifton, Lula Perkins, Edna Starks Hicks and Frances Hammond. *Courtesy of Jean Clifton Sharon*

Employees of Starks' Headache Powder, circa 1940. From left to right: Lucy Bethel Holt, Dora Clifton, Frances Fain, Sara Jane Osborne, Frances Hammond and Lula Perkins. Edna Starks Hicks is sitting in front. *Courtesy of Jean Clifton Sharon*

Lexington rooftops looking northwest, 1947. Included are the federal courthouse and St. Peter Catholic Church. *Courtesy of Lexington History Museum*

John P. Boyd, right, with an unidentified man in the Nash dealership on West Main Street, circa 1950. *Courtesy of Betty Boyd*

Royal Palm passenger train leaving the Georgetown station, circa 1950. *Courtesy of Georgetown and Scott County Historical Society*

Jack Carroll, left, and Asa Parker, 1952. Mr. Parker drove for Dance Trucking Company. *Courtesy of Gwendolyn Griffith Powell*

Georgetown Laundry on Main Street, 1950. *Courtesy of Georgetown and Scott County Historical Society*

Threshing wheat on the Caveland farm in Clark County, Combs Ferry Pike near Becknerville, June 1953. William M. Jones Jr. was owner of the J.I. Case 65-horse-power steam engine and Case separator with "Wick" Jones the engineer. *Courtesy of Lexington History Museum*

Chesapeake and Ohio railway train No. 23 passing Netherland yard office and entering the double track on the way to Union Station, circa 1950. The telegraph operator at the corner of the station is ready to hand up orders to the fireman. *Courtesy of Marion Eldridge*

Kyle White with his Farmall Cub preparing to plow his tobacco field in Nonesuch, 1952. *Courtesy of Jack A. White*

Joyland Restaurant, North Broadway and Loudon Avenue, circa 1955. The rail car No. 311 was the last interurban purchased by the Kentucky Traction & Terminal Co. It operated between Lexington and the surrounding communities until abandonment, January 1934. *Courtesy of Marion Eldridge*

Union Station railroad yards and Vine Street looking west from the viaduct, 1956. *Courtesy of University of Kentucky Libraries 1.11-3421.01*

Keene Springs Hotel, Keene, circa 1955. *Courtesy of Jessamine County Historical Society*

Advertisement for Shell gasoline, circa 1955. *Courtesy of Georgetown and Scott County Historical Society*

Tobacco sale warehouse, circa 1960. *Courtesy of Lexington History Museum*

Louisville & Nashville railroad depot at Avon, circa 1953, was originally the depot for the Lexington & Eastern railway. *Courtesy of Marion Eldridge*

The
Renfrew House

MENU

3 Miles North of Harrodsburg on U.S. 68
Turn Left Onto Curry Pike, 1½ Miles to
The Renfrew House
Dial 734-4291 — Harrodsburg, Ky.

Tobacco sale, circa 1960. *Courtesy of Lexington History Museum*

Menu from the Renfrew House, circa 1955. Bob Renfrew owned and operated the restaurant, popular for group parties during that time. He was also the original restaurateur at Shakertown. *Courtesy of Lou and Mary Beth Noel*

Drug store in Georgetown, March 1961. Front to back: Bernice Thompson, Barbara Earl Friedly, Geneve (unknown) and Irene (unknown). *Courtesy of Georgetown and Scott County Historical Society*

Threshing wheat in Jessamine County, 1958. Charlie Wilson and Vernon Johnson are on top of the equipment that was owned by Cecil and Vernon Johnson. *Courtesy of Howard C. Teater*

Harold F. Lee owned and operated a small engine repair shop in Versailles in the 1960s. *Courtesy of Harold W. Lee*

West Short Street between Upper and Limestone streets, Lexington, 1961. The Standard Furniture Co. store was built in 1889 and razed in February 1962. *Courtesy of Transylvania University Library, J. Winston Coleman Jr. Collection*

The Ben Ali theater on East Main Street opposite the Phoenix Hotel. The building was razed the winter of 1964-65. *Courtesy of Transylvania University Library, J. Winston Coleman Jr. Collection*

IBM plant, circa 1965. *Courtesy of Lexington History Museum*

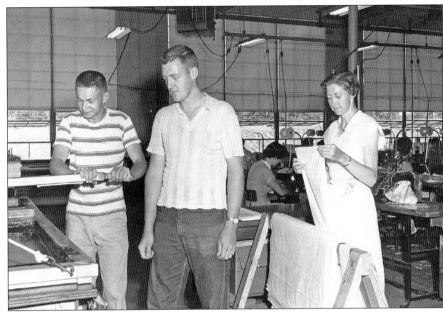

Workers at the Electric Parts factory in Georgetown, circa 1965. *Courtesy of Georgetown and Scott County Historical Society*

Cutting tobacco, Fayette County, 1969. *Courtesy of Transylvania University Library, J. Winston Coleman Jr. Collection*

Working the tobacco field in Fayette County, circa 1965. *Courtesy of Transylvania University Library, J. Winston Coleman Jr. Collection*

PUBLIC SERVICE

There's something about a man — or a woman — in uniform. The decades covered here start with World War II, and there are plenty of photos of what has been called "the Greatest Generation." Cameras of the early 1940s captured image after image of young men about to leave the security of Central Kentucky for unknown dangers in Europe and Asia – and even a scene of soldiers who were passing through town dancing with local young women at a "stopover station" dance pavilion.

There also are nurses, policemen, fire-fighters and crossing guards. Note the several photos of motorcycle cops; they seemed to draw photographers' attention.

Lexington was becoming a city large enough to attract national political figures, and even movie stars. Here is President Eisenhower, in the back of a Cadillac, and soon-to-be-President Kennedy, riding down Main Street in a Chevrolet convertible on a campaign stop. President Johnson was here to receive an honorary diploma from the University of Kentucky. Would-be-presidents Robert F. Kennedy, Eugene McCarthy and George Wallace made stops (and a black Lexington police lieutenant was assigned to protect the segregationist Alabama governor).

Martin Luther King Jr. made a speech in Frankfort, Lady Bird Johnson stumped for her husband and Rose Kennedy for her son, and Margaret Truman made a whistle stop.

Lexington Police motorcycle officers, left to right: Bill Foster, Bryan Henry, Lloyd Lindsey and Claude Ginter getting ready to hit the streets, Nov. 15, 1950. *Courtesy of Lexington Public Safety Museum*

Safety Boy Patrol signs on the courthouse lawn, Oct. 28, 1940. Slower driving was promoted in this campaign to increase student safety through the installation of these safety boy signs on roads near Fayette County schools. Their purpose was to remind drivers, as Chief of Fayette County Police J.W. McChord advertised in the *Lexington Leader*, that "recklessness, carelessness, thoughtlessness, fast driving and plain old every day discourtesy cause most of the accidents." The officials active in the campaign, left to right: Louis Rives, County Magistrate; H.D. Coleman, patrol captain; Charles B. Fentress Jr., patrolman; Judge W.E. Nichols and W.C. Uhlman, Kentucky Peace Officers Association. *Courtesy of Lexington Public Safety Museum*

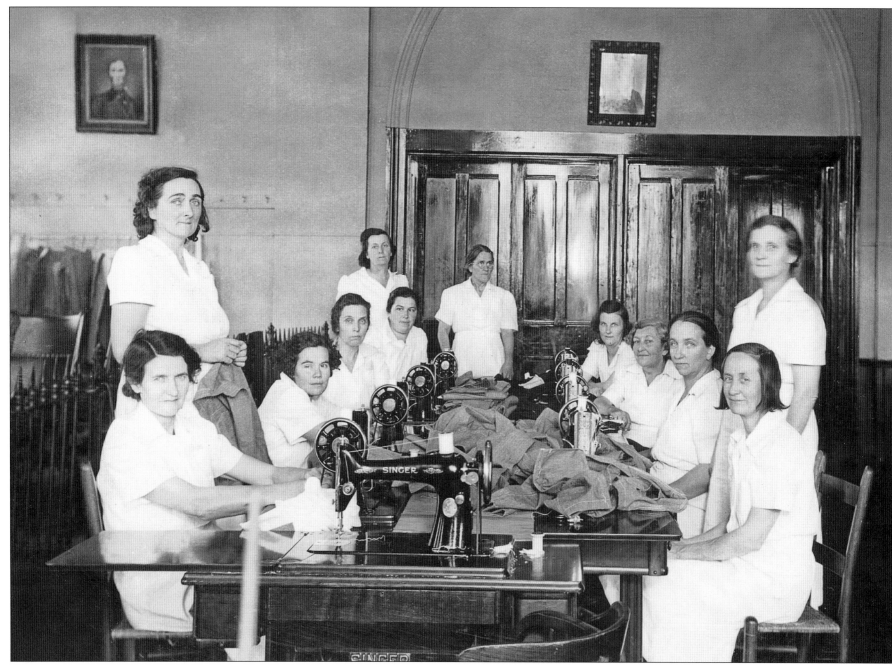

WPA sewing unit did its work at the Woodford County Courthouse when court was not in session, circa 1940. Standing on the left is Mrs. Carter and on the right is Mrs. Wilson. *Courtesy of Woodford County Historical Society*

Red Cross Volunteer Nurses Aide Corps members being given their 150-hour service stripes, 1942. Left to right: Mrs. O.D. Boots, Mrs. J.E. Humphrey, Mrs. L.W. Prewitt and Mrs. S.R. McCall. *Courtesy of Jim Humphrey*

George Fritz of Lexington served in the Army Allied Forces during World War II starting in Africa and moving up through Italy. He served 42 months. This photograph was taken in Rome on Dec. 8, 1944, and mailed home to his sweetheart, who later became his wife, as a Christmas present. *Courtesy of George F. Fritz*

William L. Heizer Jr. with his mother, Mrs. W.L. Heizer, during World War II, 1941. William's father was a physician in Lexington from 1918 until his death in 1938. William became a physician after the war and practiced in Lexington. *Courtesy of Lucien H. Rice*

Paul Adams, home on leave from the Navy during World War II, with little brother David. *Courtesy of Frank and Joy Fugazzi*

Lexington Fire Department members, circa 1942, left to right: Hargus Maness, unidentified, Joe Preston and unidentified. *Courtesy of Lexington Public Safety Museum*

John P. Boyd, left, with an unidentified friend on the University of Kentucky campus, 1943. The university housed the Army Specialized Training Program during World War II. *Courtesy of Betty Boyd*

Christine Needham Massie and Joseph Logan Massie before Joe left for the Philippines during World War II. *Courtesy of Carol Needham Massie*

Two Adams brothers home on leave during World War II. Jim, left, served in the Marine Corps; Paul served in the Navy. *Courtesy of Frank and Joy Fugazzi*

Army Pfc. William B. Burdett while in Germany, 1944. *Courtesy of Lillian B. Perkins*

Frank Fugazzi, Marine Corps, on a troop ship going to Korea, November 1950. During World War II he served in the Navy on a landing ship tank. *Courtesy of Frank and Joy Fugazzi*

An Army B-52 bomber was the first big plane to land at the new Blue Grass airport on Versailles Road, July 11, 1942. *Courtesy of University of Kentucky Libraries 1.13-35.07*

William Carrick James, left, with an unidentified friend during service in England, circa 1944. *Courtesy of Georgetown and Scott County Historical Society*

Banquet celebrating the end of World War II at Bethesda Baptist Church, 1945. Left to right: Mayme Hayes, Rev. L.J. Johnson, Lucy Hart Smith, Asbury Scott, Louis Hill and Ethel Hayes. *Courtesy of Betty Yates Smithers*

Servicemen and a Red Cross worker aboard the presidential yacht *Williamsburg*. The yacht was turned over to the American Red Cross for providing one-day cruises down the Potomac River for wounded servicemen. The president designated the *Williamsburg* as a recreation ship to express "the feeling of appreciation and gratitude which the people of this country owe to the members of their armed forces." Manned by a U.S. Navy crew, the craft made twice-weekly trips carrying 50 ambulatory patients from nearby military hospitals on each cruise. Red Cross provided drivers and transportation to shipside, and volunteers accompanied the servicemen on each cruise. PFC Joseph L. Slugantz of Nicholasville is seated fourth from the right. *Courtesy of Jessamine County Historical Society*

Gambling equipment recovered from a raid in Scott County, July 1948. *Courtesy of Georgetown and Scott County Historical Society*

Lexington Police Officer J. Harrison Sallee writing a citation, July 9, 1946. *Courtesy of Lexington Public Safety Museum*

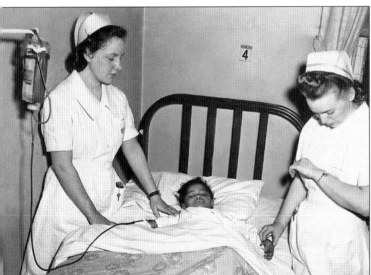

The first unit of war surplus blood plasma given in Lexington was administered at St. Joseph Hospital to a young burn patient in 1945. Student nurses attending were Mary Ellen Amato, left, and Mary Kelly. *Courtesy of Mary Ellen Amato*

Behind police headquarters, 140 Walnut St., circa 1945. Traffic motorcycle officers, left to right: Bill Sellers, Herman Hensley, William Jordan, Louis Kirby and Austin B. Price. *Courtesy of Lexington Public Safety Museum*

Lexington Police Department's Second Platoon standing on the steps to the Municipal Building, 136-140 Walnut St., Aug. 5, 1947. Standing in the front row left to right: Sgt. James W. "Jimmy" Glass, Assistant Chief Austin B. Price and Lieutenant Zac A. Carter. Second row: Pete Hannon, Jesse Williams, unidentified unidentified, unidentified and James W. Blankenship. Third row: William "Bill" G. Sellers, L. Meyers, unidentified and Wallace McMurray. Back row: unidentified and Bill Foster. *Courtesy of Lexington Public Safety Museum*

Servicemen dancing at the stopover station dance pavilion at the north end of Esplanade, June 23, 1944. *Courtesy of University of Kentucky Libraries 1.13-362.01*

Margaret Truman, daughter of President Harry Truman, is helped off the train in Lexington the day before the Kentucky Derby, May 3, 1946. *Courtesy of University of Kentucky Libraries 1.13-64.05*

Lexington patrolman Lloyd Lindsey watches as two city workhouse prisoners pour confiscated moonshine whiskey into the sewer, Jan. 11, 1951. *Courtesy of University of Kentucky Libraries 1.106-67*

Carl G. Richardson, left, with his sister, Katherine Richardson Lee, and her husband, Harold F. Lee, Woodford County, circa 1945. *Courtesy of Harold W. Lee*

Margie Cropper volunteered as a nurse aide at Good Samaritan Hospital, 1944. *Courtesy of Harold and Marjorie Easley*

Control center and switchboard at the U.S. Public Health Service Hospital on Leestown Road, February 1961. From left to right: Betty Jo Hoskins, Clyde Hall and Joy Adams Fugazzi. *Courtesy of Frank and Joy Fugazzi*

Nicholasville women at a hospital in Lexington, circa 1950. On the right are Virginia Rose, Kathleen Jennette and Rachel Arnold. *Courtesy of Jessamine County Historical Society*

Kentucky National Guard Headquarters Battalion 23 Corps Artillery, Kentucky National Guard, 1955. Left to right: Donald Chumley, John McFadden, Joseph McFadden and Henry Bell. *Courtesy of Donald Chumley*

Thomas E. Smithers, age 17, in the U.S. Army, 1951. He served five years in the Army and another five years in the reserves. *Courtesy of Betty Yates Smithers*

Lexington Fire Department members, circa 1952, left to right: J.C. "Jay" Tunstill, an unidentified man at the wheel and Buford Craft. They are in front of Fire Station No. 5 on Woodland and Maxwell streets. *Courtesy of June H. Tunstill*

Lexington Traffic School Guard Division was formed to assist with children crossing the streets around local schools. Mrs. Louise Childers was made president. Traffic Sergeant Joseph Modica organized and trained the newly-formed unit. Front row, left to right: Mayor Fred Fugazzi, Dorothy Dickens, Louise Childers, Christine Walker, unidentified and Assistant Chief Guy W. Maupin. Second row: Emily Hay, Opal Nolan, Mary Woodridge, Lois Carter and Amanda Elliott. Third row: Assistant Chief E.C. Hall, Jane Hawthorn, unidentified, unidentified, Josephine Hatchett and Captain William Clancy. Back row: Sergeant Joseph A. Modica, Christine Stubbler, unidentified, Grace Rogers and unidentified. *Courtesy of Lexington Public Safety Museum*

William "Stinky" Davis, Bryan Henry, Bill Foster, Lloyd Lindsey behind *Wizard of Oz* actress Judy Garland, Espy Hedger, Hobert Carey and John Doyle, circa 1953. *Courtesy of Lexington Public Safety Museum*

61st Special Infantry Co., Marine Corps, Lexington, during summer training at Camp Lejeune, N.C., 1954. Maj. Gus T. Petro, fourth from the right in the front row, was the commanding officer. Frank Fugazzi is first on the left in the second row. *Courtesy of Frank and Joy Fugazzi*

John B. Breckinridge delegates gathered outside the Fayette County Courthouse after being locked out by the A.B. "Happy" Chandler supporters during the candidate selection process, circa 1955. *Courtesy of Lexington History Museum*

St. Joseph Hospital Nazareth School of Nursing capping ceremony, Feb. 24, 1956. *Courtesy of Donald Chumley*

A rookie policeman directs traffic under the watchful eye of his training officer, John Hiten, at the corner of West Main Street and Jefferson Street, circa 1957. *Courtesy of Lexington Public Safety Museum*

President Eisenhower on his visit to Lexington, October 1956. The motorcade is leaving the airport to head downtown. A group of fourth- and fifth-grade students from Margaret Hall School are in the front center of the crowd. *Courtesy of Fran Allen*

Mayors of Lexington and Deauville, France, 1956, unveiling a marker at the city limits declaring their cities the first of four sister city relationship established by Lexington. *Courtesy of Lexington History Museum*

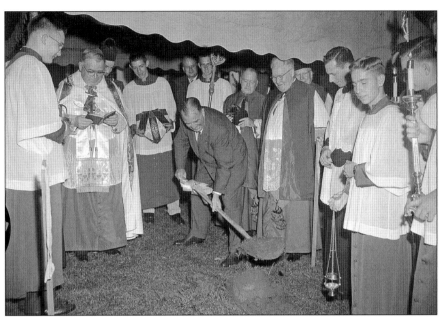

Gov. A.B. "Happy" Chandler breaks ground for the new St. Joseph Hospital, October 1956. *Courtesy of University of Kentucky Libraries 1.11-2618.01*

Gov. A.B. "Happy" Chandler during ground-breaking ceremonies for the University of Kentucky's Chandler Medical Center, December 1957. *Courtesy of University of Kentucky Libraries 1.12-3190.04*

Cleaning up after a cross burning in Woodland Park, summer of 1960. *Courtesy of Donald Chumley*

Lexington Police motorcycle officers, left to right: Albert Meredith, Ray Wright and Stanley "Bud" Hornbeck, 1957. *Courtesy of Donald Chumley*

The University of Kentucky win over the University of Tennessee football team, Nov. 23, 1959, resulted in nine students arrested and four people injured, including a policeman and fireman. Gov. A.B. "Happy" Chandler declared the upcoming Wednesday a holiday, giving a five-day Thanksgiving vacation. The University voted "no" on the holiday. Others marched down to City Hall on Walnut Street to take control and break them out. The 3,000 protesting students slowly dispersed and went back to campus shortly after a speech given by Chief E.C. Hale. *Courtesy of Lexington Public Safety Museum*

Lexington Police Department before it merged with the Fayette County Police Department, circa 1960. Officers are on the steps of St. Peter Catholic Church on Barr Street. *Courtesy of Donald Chumley*

The Rev. Martin Luther King Jr. spoke in Frankfort in front of the State Capitol, March 5, 1964. *Courtesy of University of Kentucky Libraries V.628C*

Lady Bird Johnson, left, wife of Democratic vice-pesidental candidate Lyndon Johnson, and Rose Kennedy, mother of presidential candidate John Kennedy, greet voters at a reception at the Phoenix Hotel in Lexington during the run-up to the 1960 election, Oct. 3, 1960. *Courtesy of University of Kentucky Libraries R.2426E*

Lexington Fire Department Vogt Reel House on Jefferson Street, circa 1960. From left to right: P. Green, unidentified, Lewis Farmer, A. Carter, C. Dugger and D. Wison.

Courtesy of Lexington Public Safety Museum

John F. Kennedy riding in a parade on Main Street during his presidential campaign, October 1960. *Courtesy of Lexington History Museum*

Candy Stripers at Woodford Memorial Hospital in front of a temporary office during the remodeling of the hospital, Versailles, 1963. Front row, left to right: Lynn Perkins, Nancy Lewis, Patti Lane, Phyllis Britton, Charlene Updike, Mary Dan Karsner, Renee Reeves, Barbara Jo Gibson, Cornelia Tilghman, Libby Tilghman, Sondra Shields, Susie Shotwell and Ruth Ann Evans. Back row: Rebecca Montgomery, Sarann Shepherd, Jo Ann Fremont, Judy Heinig, Pam Dearinger, Kay Watts, Janice Spalding, Pat Dunlap, Donna Semones, Molly Cleveland, Fran Fishback, Wanda Cornish, Jo Della Neace and Bonnie Bradshaw. *Courtesy of Kevin Lane Dearinger and Fran Allen*

The Woodford County Courthouse was destroyed by fire on Oct. 11, 1965. This was the third courthouse to stand on the same property in downtown Versailles. *Courtesy of Woodford County Historical Society*

Scott County Courthouse, circa 1965. *Courtesy of Georgetown and Scott County Historical Society*

U.S. President Lyndon Johnson receiving The Centennial Honorary Degree of Doctor of Laws from the University of Kentucky, Feb. 22, 1965. Kentucky Gov. Edward T. Breathitt is draping the academic hood around the President. *Courtesy of University of Kentucky Libraries W.447J*

Demonstrators against the Vietnam War marching outside of University of Kentucky Memorial Coliseum, February 1966. *Courtesy of University of Kentucky Libraries X.427D*

U.S. Sen. Robert Kennedy greets supporters as he arrives at Blue Grass Field for a tour of Eastern Kentucky during his campaign for president, Feb. 13, 1968. *Courtesy of University of Kentucky Libraries X.427D*

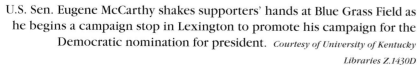

Lt. James Perkins, left, of the Lexington Police Department guarding Alabama Governor George Wallace during a visit to Lexington, 1968. *Courtesy of Lillian B. Perkins*

U.S. Sen. Eugene McCarthy shakes supporters' hands at Blue Grass Field as he begins a campaign stop in Lexington to promote his campaign for the Democratic nomination for president. *Courtesy of University of Kentucky Libraries Z.1430D*

CLUBS & ORGANIZATIONS

People in Lexington and surrounding towns have long been joiners. The clubs and organizations they formed help shape the community and provide a sense of belonging in a time of rapid population growth and social change.

Photos in this section range from Boy Scouts to Homemakers clubs.

There is the Central Kentucky Youth Orchestra, founded in 1948 and still going strong. In 1963, the orchestra made it all the way to the White House lawn. That handsome man standing in front of the orchestra is President Kennedy.

There are the boys in Future Farmers of America, nervously awaiting the judging of their cattle in Versailles, Future Homemakers of America decked out in gowns for a state banquet in Morehead, and a leggy shot of the Lexington Women's Club Follies from the mid-1950s.

This section also includes no fewer than three photos of Business and Professional Woman's Club, a sure sign that the role of women in society was changing.

Homemakers dinner, Georgetown, 1956. *Courtesy of Georgetown and Scott County Historical Society*

Clio Club, Nicholasville, 1943. Front row, left to right: Mrs. John Von Grunigen, Miss Annasteele Taylor, Mrs. William Woods, Mrs. H.B. Taylor, Mrs. Jeannette Combs, Mrs. Norton Fitch and Mrs. Sam Price. Second row: Mrs. Robert Denny, Mrs. Andrew Hemphill, Miss Lena Breiner, Mrs. Sam Steenberger and Mrs. Marvin Pentz. Third row: Mrs. Paul Simpson, Mrs. Wallace Wharton, Mrs. L.V. Williams, Mrs. Robert Simpson and Mrs. William B. Hoover. *Courtesy of Jessamine County Historical Society*

Versailles Future Farmers of America judging cattle on Court Street, 1944. Maurice Guy Currens is on the left in front of the sign on the truck. Other FFA members included are: Randolph Cotton, Jack Etherington, Bobby Boston, Cecil Smith, Edward Collins, Roy Collins and Joe Etherington. *Courtesy of Joyce Olson Currens*

Boy Scout Troop 4 from Central Christian Church on clean-up day at 110 Hamilton Park off Versailles Road, circa 1946. Bruce Poundstone, right, is scoutmaster. Fourth from the right is Jim Humphrey, senior patrol leader. *Courtesy of Jim Humphrey*

Lexington Chamber of Commerce men on a train, circa 1946. The group was traveling to another community to learn about its chamber activities. The man on the left with the smile is Sterling T. Chase, president of the Lexington Chamber of Commerce. *Courtesy of Mary Jo Chase Burke and Pat Chase Corman*

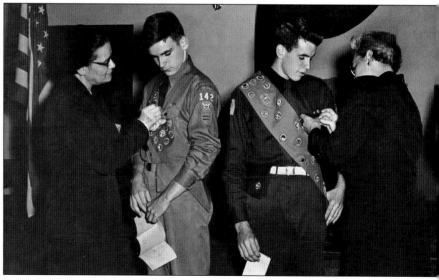

Eagle Scout ceremony at First Methodist Church, Morehead, 1951. From left to right: Mary Young with her son Don and Lucien Rice with his mother Virginia. Lucien and his brother, Bill, were among the first brothers to achieve the Eagle Scout award in Rowan County. *Courtesy of Lucien H. Rice*

Lena Madesin Phillips Business and Professional Women's Club, Nicholasville, circa 1950. Front row, left to right: Virginia Dobbs, Bertha Walter, Evalene Sears, Mary Lou Guyn, Hallie Cox, Kate Woods, Anna Price and Frances Adams. Also included are: Bonnie Jarrat, Emma Logan Boggs, Mary Alice Boggs, Esther Hervey, Hester Woods, Nona Christine Suell, Lavern Tanner, Mrs. A. Stainbock, Mrs. Sutherland, Eleanor Blakeman, Dorothy Ward, Frances Ward, Alice Hughes, Margaret H. Brumfield, Clara Latimer, Frances Dobbs, Mary Tom Moynahan, Mattie Mae Glass, Gertrude Watts, Nellie McDowell, Louise Dickerson, Nora Jane Ison and Rosa Lena Brumfield. *Courtesy of Jessamine County Historical Society*

Mes Cheri social club having a formal dance at the Paradise Inn, 1958. Left to right: Pauline Harris, Marylyn Henderson, Lillian Howard, Katie Greene, Augustine Douglas, Carolyn Allen, Anna Jackson, Pearlina Holman, Marjorie Taylor and Marcella Bush. *Courtesy of Lillian B. Perkins*

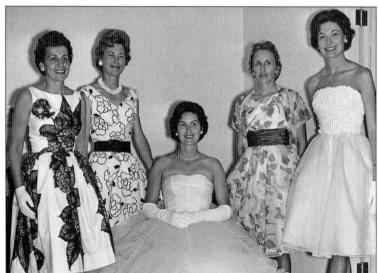

Style show presented by the American Home Department of the Lexington Women's Club, May 1962. From left to right: Mrs. Edward Hodgetts, Mrs. Claude Terrell, Mrs. Lloyd Waddell, Mrs. Raymond Jordan and Mrs. Kenneth Fortune. *Courtesy of Opal Hall Waddell*

Labor Day motorists heading south through Nicholasville were given a coffee break on wheels by members of the Business and Professional Women's Club, 1961. They were promoting the slogan of the Department of Public Safety, "For safety's sake, take a coffee break." *Courtesy of Jessamine County Historical Society*

Lexington Women's Club Follies, 1954. *Courtesy of Mary Lynn Sanders Turley*

Boy Scout Troop 89 sponsored by First Presbyterian Church on a campout, 1961. *Courtesy of Lucien H. Rice*

Central Kentucky Youth Symphony Orchestra performing at McAlister Auditorium on the Transylvania University campus, circa 1962. The floor, which was used for playing basketball as well, was covered to protect it. Joe Pival is the orchestra's conductor. Included in the orchestra are Michael and Jeanne Anne Jones, children of the orchestra's business manager, Miriam Jones. Michael played in the first violin section; Jeanne Anne in the second violin section. *Courtesy of Miriam Lamy Jones Woolfolk*

Boy Scout Troop 30 at Arlington Christian Church, 1960. Scouter Lucien H. Rice is standing on the left. George Vise is third from the right in the front row. Fourth from the left in the back row is Cecil Smith, who was Fayette County's Santa Claus for many years. *Courtesy of Lucien H. Rice*

Officers of Scott County Business and Professional Women's Club, May 28, 1968, left to right: Helen Kain, Norma J. True, Marcella Johnson, Mary Bettie Martin, Marguerite Carr, Alice R. Leach, Mrs. Glenwood Williams, Mildred Adamczyk and Edna Jones. *Courtesy of Georgetown and Scott County Historical Society*

Woodford County Cadet Band on the stage of Versailles High School, circa 1960. The band director was Dexter Marsh. *Courtesy of Harold W. Lee*

Central Kentucky Youth Symphony Orchestra performing on the White House Lawn, 1963. Conductor Joseph Pival is standing behind President John F. Kennedy. This photograph was taken by the orchestra's business manager, Miriam Jones, with a Brownie camera from her seat in the front row. Orchestra members include, on violins: Mary Jo Anderson, Susanne Bolender, Amy Boyarsky, Lois Bradley, Ann Bridges, Cornelia Colyer, Rex Conner, Patricia Coombs, Susan Cross, Robert Core, Pamela Drennon, Paula Erwin, Robert Fleishman, Sandra Freels, Joseph Gatwood, Mary Margaret Heaton, Montez Henderson, Kathleen Hopkins, Michael Jones, Jeanne Jones, Brenda Layman, Catherine McGlasson, Carolyn Plummer, Niel Plummer, Mary Bowman Ringo, Sharon Sue Smith, Willis A. Sutton, Susan Taylor, Cara Williams and Michele Wright. Violas: Anne Core, Martha Daily, Mary Ellen Craft, Rebecca DeBoer, Mary Kanner, Darliene Moore, Kathryn Plummer and Patricia Young. Cellos: Gene Attkisson, Kathleen Dicken, Marsha Sue Craft, Joan Hixson, Ann McGuire, Paige Prewitt, Mary Warfield, Kathleen Warford and Wendi Wright. Basses: Anna Bruce Neal, Sharon Lou Smith and David Thompson. Flutes: Catherine Allison, Beth Blount, Sharon Gabby, Anne Marlowe and Rebecca Reid. Oboes: Charles Barrett, Mary Gail Engle, Donna Haydon, Pamela Schisler and Katherine Sparks. Bassoons: Nancy Engle, Paula Shane and Diana Vicky Smith. Clarinets: Henrietta Efkeman, Timothy Hill, Janice George and William Johnson. Trumpets: John Burrows, Thomas Brawner, Charles Neal and William Foster. French Horns: Jerry Bootze, Frederick Irtz, Robert Osborne, Robin Reed and Lee Townsend. Trombones: Nicolas Bentley, Kenneth Combs, James Hughbanks and Robert Kleinschmidt. Percussion: David Austin, Robert Cobb and Kim McCrary. The tuba was played by James L. Combs. Larry Beach was their student manager. The orchestra was organized in 1948. From an initial group of 14 string players, it mushroomed into a full symphony. *Courtesy of Miriam Lamy Jones Woolfolk*

RELIGION

Religion has always played an important role in the lives of the people of Central Kentucky, and it appeared to be especially strong in the 1940s, '50s and '60s.

Here we have the smiling faces of Vacation Bible School classes, and a large group of children moving from the beginner to the primary level in a Sunday school class. They even have mortar boards and graduation certificates.

There are photos of Young Ambassadors, and Rainbow Girls, and a stern line of church deacons.

Sometimes, entire congregations would sit for a photo, with everyone wearing their Sunday best. Those photos show that then, as now, Lexington is seldom so segregated as when we gather in our separate places of worship.

Eighth-grade graduating class of St. Leo's School at St. Leo's Church in Versailles, 1964. Front row, left to right: Kevin Lane Dearinger, head altar boy; David Bernard Dearinger; Phyllis Printers; Lois Mulry; Michael Canty and Michael Dotson, altar boy. Back row: Pam Espin, Susie Kitchen, Carol Schoo, Gail Yount and Pam Gilkerson. The teacher is Sister Alma Joseph. *Courtesy of Kevin Lane Dearinger*

Vacation Bible School at Clear Creek Baptist Church, Woodford County, circa 1942. Lillie Tilghman is second from the right in the front row. Her mother, Alice Tilghman, is the third person from the right in the back. *Courtesy of Lillie Tilghman Cox*

Rainbow Girls Sunday school at Midway Baptist Church, 1943. Included are: Joyce Noel, Jean Clifton, Gladys Riddle, Doris Merriman, Mary Wagner, Doris Bain, Helen Bush, Margaret Maye, Flora Rawlings, Lily White, Louise Hill, Dorothy Sames, Ruth Wash, Syble Long, Lucy Wagner and Mildred Harmon. *Courtesy of Jean Clifton Sharon*

Mrs. J.E. Humphrey giving diplomas to members of the Royal Ambassadors from Calvary Baptist Church, circa 1948. *Courtesy of Jim Humphrey*

Congregation leaving Epworth Methodist Church, 1015 N. Limestone St., after Sunday services, circa 1952. *Courtesy of June H. Tunstill*

Vacation Bible School from Epworth Methodist Church visiting the Lexington Fire Department, 1950. *Courtesy of June H. Tunstill*

Epworth Methodist Church at 1015 N. Limestone St. shortly before the congregation moved in on the first Sunday of October, 1950. *Courtesy of June H. Tunstill*

Sunday school class from Epworth Methodist Church, circa 1955. *Courtesy of June H. Tunstill*

Millville Baptist Church deacons, circa 1955, from left to right: Pastor Hinson, unidentified, Dorsey Caudle, unidentified, Harry Franklin Hippe, unidentified, Ed Knight and Bob Etherington. *Courtesy of Lillie Tilghman Cox*

Bethesda Baptist Church congregation, 1942. Rev. Levi Johnson was the pastor. Third from the left in the front row is Betty Yates. *Courtesy of Betty Yates Smithers*

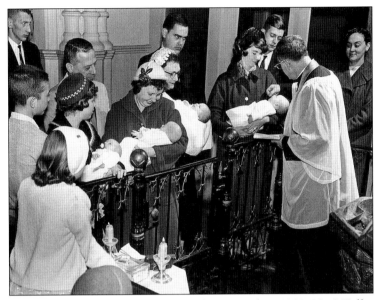

Baptism at St. Paul Catholic Church, November 1959. Mari Kelly, daughter of Donald and Alyce Chumley, is the baby on the right. *Courtesy of Donald Chumley*

Vacation Bible School of Versailles Baptist Church, circa 1960. *Courtesy of Harold W. Lee*

First board of Elkhorn Baptist Community Center on West High Street, circa 1965. Included are: director Anne Davis, Mrs. Encil Deen, Rev. Donald White, Irene Heathman, Pat Corman, Julia Woodward, Mrs. Kuhnle, William Griffin, Rev. Franklin Owen, Byrd Ison and Mr. Wells. *Courtesy of Pat Chase Corman*

Graduation from beginner to primary Sunday school class at Grace Baptist Church, 1955. Pat Ritchey is fourth from the right in the front row. Others included are: Susan Reams, Billy Strain, Andy Shuping, Ronnie Oliver, Mrs. Pennabaker and Mrs. Farris. *Courtesy of Pat Ritchey*

Congregation of St. Francis Catholic Church. *Courtesy of Georgetown and Scott County Historical Society*

Confirmation day at St. Leo's School, North Main Street, Versailles, May 16, 1961. David Dearinger was one of the confirmands. *Courtesy of David Dearinger*

Midway Baptist Church Vacation Bible School, July 1964. First row, left to right: Brent Littrell, Cindy Sharon, Sheri Baker, Jeffrey Sames and Lisa Cloyd. Second row: unidentified, unidentified, Chuck Logan, unidentified, Mary Ellen Pittman, Carla Noel and Chuck Smith. *Courtesy of Libby Sharon Warfield*

St. Francis Catholic Church. *Courtesy of Georgetown and Scott County Historical Society*

EDUCATION

A h, school days. The scenes captured here run the gamut from first graders on see-saws to sorority sisters chilling at the University of Kentucky, to a decidedly older group of former Jessamine Female Institute students attending a reunion.

There's an elementary school band, and a class on a spring picnic outing.

Some of the photos are casual, but some probably were taken on picture days, which often meant deciding the night before on just the right dress or shirt that would preserve your best look for posterity.

Also captured are some unusual schools. There are students in a school for hair design, styling wigs under the watchful eyes of instructors, and girls from the Lexington School of Calculating, operating machines called comptometers.

And how's this for an oddity: A group shot from Big Picadome School, which boasted 15 sets of twins.

As in the Religion section of this book, segregation was apparent. The graduating class at Bryan Station High School in 1940 was all white. The Dunbar High School graduating class of 1945 was all African-American. But in 1958, a sign of change: A first-grade class from Midway was integrated for the first time, with four black faces sprinkled among the whites.

Dunbar High School graduating class, 1945. Mr. Baker and Mrs. Taylor were their teachers. *Courtesy of Lillian B. Perkins*

Graduating class at Bryan Station High School, circa 1940. *Courtesy of Pat Ritchey*

Great Crossing School Chapter of the Future Farmers of America, 1940-41. Included are: teacher Mr. Bales, Paul Simon, Arnold Sams, Pete McDonald, Zip Kettering, W.O. Claxon, Douglas Carr, Billy Glass, (unknown) Hixson and L.D. Parks. *Courtesy of James and Helen Carr*

Mrs. Day's kindergarten class of Little Picadome School, 1941. Student include: Helen Johnson, Sara Wells, Lanny Gregory, Alan B. Long and Ella Gene Johnson. *Courtesy of James and Helen Carr*

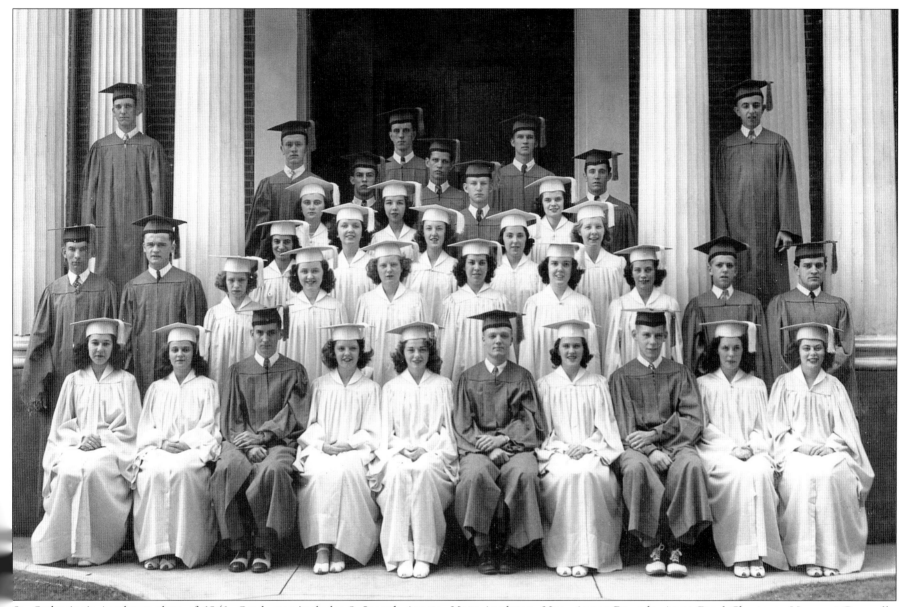

St. Catherine's Academy class of 1941. Graduates include: S. Joseph Amato, Mary Appleton, Mary Agnes Bounds, Anna Pearl Chasteen, Margaret Donnelly Concannon, Mary Ann Demma, Daniel Louis Eberhardt, Mary Catherine Egalite, Anne Frances Foley, Mary Catherine Foley, George Francis Fritz, Joseph Franz, Irene Cecilia Geran, Marjorie King, George Holtby Kinnaird, Marguerite Gloria Keene, James William Lenihan, Mary Dan Lynch, Clare Maguire, Norbert Maguire, Nina Mangione, Teresa Jane Mann, James Mahoney, Betty Lynn Matlack, Alice Juanita Murphy, John O'Neill Morgan, Miles McMenama, Margaret Ann Sallee, Mary Ellen Sheehy, Alphonso Stanonis, Ralph Sherlock, Reed Stevens, Bernard Anthony Sellman, Mary Charles Wood, Jean White, Harold William Wurtenberger and Scott Yellman. *Courtesy of George F. Fritz*

Members of the Dramatic Club at Douglass Junior High School, 1942. Front row, left to right: Virginia Howard, Lillian Burdett, Katie Thomas, Mary Hawkins, Anna Margaret Thomas, Anna Whiteside and May Smith. Second row: George Biggerstaff, Walter Milton, Annabelle Milton, Maurice Johnson, Alice Beatty, Shirley Taylor and Robert Baker. *Courtesy of Virginia H. French*

Lexington School of Calculating, 1942. They are working on comptometers that were used to add, subtract, multiply and divide. The odd numbers on the keyboard were concave; the even numbers were smooth. Berniece Combs, the teacher, is standing on the right in the back with the flowered dress. Starting from the left near the wall and around the table: Sally Bowman, unidentified, unidentified, Carolyn Friedly, Mary Powers, unidentified, unidentified, Lucille Shotwell, Dorothy Borland and unidentified. Seated in back and around the other table: June Houston, Miss Comb's daughter, Eunice Burch, unidentified, unidentified, Ann Richmond, unidentified, unidentified, Frances Sammons, Elinor Dun, unidentified, unidentified and unidentified. The back row is unidentified. Many of the graduates worked at the Department of Agriculture in the ASCS office in the old Dudley School building. *Courtesy of June H. Tunstill*

Versailles High School, class of 1942. Front row, left to right: Clara Frances Hendricks, Joyce Curry, Jane Hogg, Mary Catherine Howard, Vivian Howard, Winnifred Hellard, J.W. Drury, Jack Hayden, Allen Johnson and L.J. Crain. Second row: Mae Curry, Thelma Adams, Mary Brown, Etta Disponette, Marion Hackney, Wanda Etherington, Marjorie Goodrich, Virginia Garter, Irene Ford and Edythe Hartley. Third row: Christine Bailey, Mary Elizabeth Carnell, Ella Mae Crowe, Hazel Hartley, Gladys Carter, Ida Maria Cosby, Mary Elizabeth Bradshaw, Edith English and Pauline Dozier. Fourth row: Homer Coatney, William Henry Chapman, Joe Farris, Philip Britton, Mrs. Tiller, Logan Brown, Alfred Owen Drury and William Atwood. Back row: Howard Hilton, Wilbur Angel, Frank James Carter, Raymond Holman, Adrian Currens, Carl Chapman and Robert Curry. *Courtesy of Woodford County Historical Society*

Lafayette High School band, 1944. The director is Harold Stocking. *Courtesy of Jim Humphrey*

Apple Pi Club of Henry Clay High School, 1945. Front row, left to right: Nancy Collis, Martha Ann Wilson, Nancy Bradford, Mary Jo Chase, Ann Kirtley, Julia Ann Hurst, Margaret Tweedy and Judith Luigart. Second row: Jerry Hinson, Anita Underhill, Nancy Lou Eden, Mary Alice Mayer, Pat Chase, Barbara Stanfill, Joan Essig, Boonie Dickston, Shelley Thompson, Betty Jane Scrivner, unidentified, Doris Coleman, Betty Elliott, Mary Ellen Price and Joan Collis. *Courtesy of Mary Jo Chase Burke, Pat Chase Corman and Lou and Mary Beth Noel*

First graders on the University Training School playground on Scott Street during recess, 1945. Included are: Hannah Hargett, Elizabeth Clark, Linda Williams, Jane Ely, Missy LeBus, Prissy Roberts and Barbara Harper. *Courtesy of Barbara Harper Bach*

Virginia Howard, left, and Lillian Burdett joining a sorority, Sigma Gamma Rho, at Kentucky State College, 1946. *Courtesy of Virginia H. French*

Young women who lived at Patterson Hall and McDowell House, University of Kentucky, 1945. There was not room in the dormitories for all the freshman so some lived in the home behind the dormitory.
Courtesy of Opal Hall Waddell

Senior homeroom students of Miss Mathews, Henry Clay High School, **1945.** *Courtesy of Mary Lynn Sanders Turley*

A student room in the Alpha Delta Pi House at the University of Kentucky, 1946. Suzanne Seeze is seated on the top bed. Below are, left to right: Mary Montague, Mary Lou Olson and Jo Ann Marsh. *Courtesy of Opal Hall Waddell*

Senior English class at Henry Clay High School, 1947, on the front porch of their teacher, Ruth Matthews', home. From left to right: Guy Weeks, David Figart, Clay Wallace, Ed Hall, Mattie Rogers, Stanley Johnstone, Mary Hal Cochran, Mickey Regan, Betty Alexander, Bill Don Grote, Archie Howard, Kinne Barnett, Betsy Bowen, Doris Coleman, Dan Hurst, Henry Simpson, Eugene Latham, Arthur Hill and Kenneth Fagan. *Courtesy of Betty Bunting*

Stan Kenton Orchestra performing at an Alpha Delta Pi dance at the Student Union, University of Kentucky, 1947. *Courtesy of Opal Hall Waddell*

Rebel Club, Henry Clay High School, 1945. *Courtesy of Mary Lynn Sanders Turley*

Phi Delta Theta dance, 1947. From left to right: Betty Williamson, Marshall McCann, Boonie Dickston, Charles Noel, Betty Catlin and Hubbard Spencer. *Courtesy of Lou and Mary Beth Noel*

Lafayette High School Honor Society, 1948. Front row, left to right: Mary Errickson, Audrey Hardin, Barbara Burns, Anne Houston, Mary Frances McCaw, Wanda Williams, Charlotte Peters and Eliza Rowland. Second row: Marilyn Kilgus, Dorothy Watkins, Doris Elliott, Betty Hinton, Geneva Yates, Ruby Berryman, Joyce Thompson, Bobbie Dean Yates, Frances Henslee and Evelyn Baker. Third row: Mary Gregg, sponsor Miss Margaret Rowbotham, Mary Lewis, Marjorie King, Bettye Deen, Nancy Moore, Nancy Morris, Lois Romanowitz, Joanne Sparks, Marcia Hornsby and Mary Jo Bishop. Back row: Bob Wilson, Andy Polites, Jimmy Humphrey, Bobby Hardin, Ed Fallon and Jimmy Crary. *Courtesy of Jim Humphrey*

Jessamine Female Institute reunion, 1947. Front row, left to right: unidentified, Elizabeth Robinson, Virginia Stoll, Mrs. Lyne, Amanda Welch, Nora Churchill, Margaret Baker, Frances Ward and Egley Cleveland. Second row: Frances Glass Smith, Alma Evans, Sallie Mars Ballard, Edna Land, Mason Tutt, Ann Denny, Norma Taylor Simpson, Daisy Williams, Hester Woods, Shirley Garrett and Esther Hervey. Third row: Martha Land, Viola Hoover, Neva Wolfe, Alice Hughes, Nan Moore, Sallie Wilds Hoover and unidentified. *Courtesy of Jessamine County Historical Society*

Junior and senior high chorus at Douglass High School. *Courtesy of Betty Yates Smithers*

Seventh grade at Carlisle High School, 1950. *Courtesy of Don J. Dampier*

The Delta Tau Delta fraternity won the All-Campus Sing at the University of Kentucky, circa 1950. First row, left to right: Charlie Patrick, Paul Nuchols, Bill Usher, unidentified and Tom Burke. Second row: unidentified, Tom Langston, Carl Lezius and unidentified. Third row: Tommy Townes, David Catron, Jim Riggs and Jack Gutermuth. Fourth row: Jerry Wagner, Herman Regan, Frank Faulkoner, Jack Tharp and unidentified. *Courtesy of Mary Jo Chase Burke*

Groups of twins from Big Picadome School in Lexington, 1949. There were an unusual number of twins attending the school during that time. Carol Lee and Carolyn Lee McHatton are on the right in the front row. *Courtesy of Carolyn Lee Cox*

Eighth-grade graduation at Pisgah Elementary School, 1951. Front row, left to right: Charles Sebree, unidentified, Norma Jean Littrell, Mary Lee Updike and Patsy Tuttle. Back row: Laquetta Claypool, Lillie Tilghman, unidentified, Granville Bunch and principal John Ambrose. *Courtesy of Lillie Tilghman Cox*

Students at Dunbar High School, Lexington, circa 1948. First row, left to right: Tilla May Lawson and Minnie Martin. Second row: Virginia Quick, Emily Coleman, Thelma Fisher, Alma Tanner, Amanda Crockett and Sara Jackson. Third row: Bernice Thomas, Rosie Lee Thomas and Marilyn Watkins. *Courtesy of DeMaris M. Duncan*

Seventh and eighth graders at St. Agatha Academy, Winchester, May 1952. Seated in the front row, left to right: David McCracken, Patricia Treadway, Shirley Daniels, Janice Daryl, Connie Westerman, Ann Gonyer, Margaret McConnell, Margaret Quisenberry, Betty Rae King, Mary Catherine Nunan and Richard Nunan. Standing in the back row: Charles Butcher, Harriette Frazier, Jane Lindsey, Ann Brooks Barnes, Charles Spurlock, Patricia Ann Kelley, Bobbie Ann Graybill, James Rucker Lewis, Betty Hays Humkey, Mary E. Haggard, Claudette Sharp and Jim Cross. *Courtesy of Arnold Edgar Watson*

University of Kentucky marching band, 1950. The director is Warren Lutz. Drum major Don Wilson, standing behind the drum on the right, would lead the
Courtesy of Jim Humphrey

Marching band on the University of Kentucky's Stoll Field, 1949. *Courtesy of Mary Jo Chase Burke*

band with his daughter, Donna, seated on the drum, on his shoulders.

Graduating class of Douglass High School, 1954. Betty Yates is second from the left in the front row. *Courtesy of Betty Yates Smithers*

Nicholasville School class of 1951-52. Front row, left to right: Danny Peel, Rose Marie Crowe, Alex Hobbs, Billy Cole, Joyce Knight, David Wells, Jerry Vanderpool, Ronald Nichols, Rosemary Waters, Carolyn Móntgomery, Joyce Fain, Jan Rose Davis and Margaret Prewitt. Second row: Marie Kelley, (unknown) Murphy, (unknown) Crutcher, William Veatch, Douglas Grant, J.C. Bourne, June Burton, Wanda Preston, Ed Hager, (unknown) Murphy, Doris Land, Bobbie Jo Cobb and Janie Barnett. Third row: Ronnie Gossett, unidentified, (unknown) Lowry, Lydia E. Land, unidentified, Dale Smith, Lemar Miller, unidentified, unidentified, Bonnie Walker and unidentified. Fourth row: unidentified, unidentified, unidentified, Bennie (unknown), Dexter (unknown), Minnie (unknown), James (unknown), Terry Hager, Puckett (unknown), Denton (unknown), Jerry Woodside and Vernon Baker. *Courtesy of Jessamine County Historical Society*

Junior class play cast from Versailles High School, 1952. Front row, left to right: Billy True, Bobbie Ritchey, Paul Beasley and Leroy Redmon. Middle row: Mary Ann Thompson, Pauline Scudder, Pat Neal, Betsy Disponett and Jane Montgomery. Back row: Laura Gormley, (unknown) Smith, Arthur Curry, Clara Ann Moore, Shirley Dunn and teacher Linda Smith. *Courtesy of Bobbie Ritchey Benson*

Formal dance at the Margaret Hall School gym, circa 1957. *Courtesy of Fran Allen*

Third graders at Versailles Elementary School, December 1952. In the front row, left to right, are Kay Tapp and Rosemary Cox. Second row: Mary Delia Bobbitt, Linda Prather, Shirley Clifton and Joyce Campbell. Kneeling in the third row are Betty Merritt and Mary Chenault. Back row: Viola Watkins, Alice Davis, Barbree Parrish, Linda Razor and Terry Johnson. *Courtesy of Rosemary C. Johnson*

Mrs. Allen's kindergarten class, Versailles, 1951-52. Front row, left to right: Genelle Reed, Molly Cleveland, Gordon Campbell, Vicki Blackburn, Libby Tilghman, Susan Alexander and Noni Arnold. Back row: Dudley Gaines, Jim Bond Lewis, Tommy Powers, Jimmy Foster, Jimmy Alexaner, Wayne Wright, Sue Hudson, Phyllis Britton and Fran Fishback. *Courtesy of Fran Allen*

First day of school in Miss Gaines' first-grade class at Versailles Elementary School, 1952. *Courtesy of Fran Allen*

Nicholasville Elementary School, 1952-53. Front row, left to right: Shelia Rose Bruner, Mary Jane Durham, Joyce Ann Rogers, Jo Ann Hager, Willie Len Odgen, John Robert Phillips, Jerry Dale Johns, Ray Reynolds, Juanita Guy, Bradley Wayne Teater, Paul Doolin and Ronald Collins. Back row: Mrs. Vernon Johnson, Eddy Cartwright, Mary Delle Thompson, Brenda Sue Woods, Suzanne Rhineheimer, Carol Jean Shearer, Glenn Ray Perkins, Lamarr Lee Miller, Wolford D. Masters and Judy Ann Durham. *Courtesy of Jessamine County Historical Society*

Cast of the Versailles High School senior class play, 1953. Front row, left to right: Mary Ann Thompson, Leroy Redmon, Bobbie Ritchey, Joe Gormley and Margaret Adams. Back row: Pauline Scudder, Richard Lemley, Clara Ann Moore, John Gormley, Bonnie Ingram, Arthur Curry, Jane Montgomery, Bob Berryman and Eunice Atwood. *Courtesy of Bobbie Ritchey Benson*

Editorial staff of the Douglass High School yearbook, 1956. *Courtesy of DeMaris M. Duncan*

University of Kentucky Phi Mu alumnae group at the Lexington Country Club, circa 1955. Second row, left to right: Edith Howerton Cox is second; Virginia Heizer Rice is third. Standing: Mary Louise Norman Phelps is first; Nellie Day Carlin Sims is fifth. *Courtesy of Lucien H. Rice*

Nicholasville High School freshman class, circa 1952. Front row, left to right: Flossie Canter, Ann Carter, Vera Ann Wallace, B. Riley, Eleanor Moss, Dorthy Moss, (unknown) Burdine, Nancy O'Hare, Joan House and Betty Land. Second row: (unknown) Calvert, Vivian Parks, (unknown) Coyle, Betty Mastin, (unknown) Tate, (unknown) Locker and (unknown) Price. Third row: Meredith Brumfield, (unknown) Reynolds, Marie Cobb, Betty Fain, (unknown) Wilson, (unknown) Brumfield, Cora Strain, (unknown) Morris and (unknown) Watts. Fourth row: Callen Guffey, Anna Shearer, (unknown) Perkins, Lorraine East, Margaret Shearer, (unknown) Davis, (unknown) Flynn, Holton West, Bobby Duncan and (unknown) Burch. Fifth row: (unknown) Eason, Esther Mulchay, (unknown) Flynn, Della Scott, Lester Reynolds, Bobbie Wylie, Raymond Cook and A.P. Schnider. Sixth row: (unknown) Cobb, Lelia Megee, Geraldine Sloan, (unknown) Hager and Margaret May. Seventh row: Dewey Walker, Oneida Peel, Rena Bowman, Juanita Carter, Jane Foster, Evelyn Dean, (unknown) Shearer, James Letcher Peel and Roy Wells. Eighth row: (unknown) Underwood, Roberta Blakeman, Chester Shearer, (unknown) Underwood, (unknown) Royse, James Belcher and Paul Preston. Left side: Rita Riley, Lelia Harris and Howard Teater. Right side: Don Evans, Don Pineur and (unknown) Fitzgerald. *Courtesy of Jessamine County Historical Society*

Versailles High School class of 1955. Front row, left to right: Vernia Goldey, Marie Kincaid, Barbara Todd, Shirley Boyd, Joan Howard, Juanita Jones, Betty Jean Hopkins, Wanda Montgomery, Geraldine Woolums, Beulah Huffman, June Joseph, Shirley Holland, Charlene Harris, Glenna Lancaster, Margaret Finnell, Patricia Brooking, Joan Tupts, Mary Frances Rose, Eleanor Routt, Betty Wilson and Marietta Foraker. Second row: teacher Miss Jessamine Mahan, Charles Blackburn, E. Leo Ginter, John Alford, Franklin Robinson, James Stanley Hughes, Phyllis Ford, Marguerite Wash, Lois Barnes, Betty Barrett, Betty Etheington, Mary Frances Cosby, Virginia Beckley Vickers, Verna Lou Crawford, Patricia Dale, Velda Redmon, Lydia McKinney, Helen Sturgeon, Barbara Perkins and Doris Grimes. Back row: teacher Earl Collins, Bill Collins, Charles Nichols, Ralph Staton, Donald Richardson, Irvin Powell, Scottie Antrobus, Floyd Roard, Horst Bolcas, Lyen Crews, Robert Coyle, Todd Williams, Glenn Poole, Sidney Cruise, William "Bill" Ahern, Charles "Tootie" McGohon, James Dozier, Jack Aldridge, Samuel Alves, Donald Semones and teacher Mrs. Earl Collins. *Courtesy of Woodford County Historical Society*

Carlisle High School, circa 1955. The school was in operation from 1893 to 1963. *Courtesy of Don J. Dampier*

St. Agatha senior class at graduation, 1956. Front row, left to right: Judy Averitt, Betty Rae King, Bobbie Ann Graybill, Claudette Ann Sharp and Patricia Ann Kelley. Back row: Harriette Frazier, Mary Catherine Nunan, Richard Elam, James Cross, Betty Hays Humkey and Margaret McConnell. *Courtesy of Arnold Edgar Watson*

Junior Prom, University High School, 1955. The women, left to right: Nancy Brown, Nancy Marr, Barbara Harper, Hannah Hargett, queen Lucy Alexander, Mary Layne Reed, Lois Weiman, Lucy Sharp and Carolyn Arnett. Men: W.R. Brown, Warley Harper, Bob Miller, Tom Rich, president Joe Hagin, Jim Ward, Hampton "Skipper" Adams, Jim Farris and Thomas Kinkead. The theme was the "Old South Ball" and was held in the gymnasium at University High School. Queen Lucy Alexander (Winchester Breathitt) later served as White House social secretary during the Nixon Administration.

Courtesy of Barbara Harper Bach

Barbara Ann's School of Dance recital at Henry Clay High School auditorium, May 27, 1955. Fran Fishback is fifth from the left, Mary Lee Slaughter is fourth from the right and Rebecca Montgomery is third from the right. *Courtesy of Fran Allen*

The first on-stage production of Irving Stone's "Love is Eternal," the story of Mary Todd Lincoln, 1956. Because Lexington was the hometown of Mary Todd, the play made its stage debut at University High School. Left to right: Barbara Harper as Ann Todd, Barbara Hymson as Mary Todd, Dudley Williams as Mr. Todd, Virginia Paul VanMeter as servant and Anne Armstrong as Mrs. Todd. *Courtesy of Barbara Harper Bach*

First-grade class from Midway High School, 1958. Front row, left to right: Elizabeth Rouse, Lea Davis, Zelma Ingulls, Bobby Door, David Warfield, Kirk Douglas Devers, Ray Murphy, Roy Jones and Lloyd Jones. Middle row: John Jones, Larry Richards, Beverly Mitchell, Libby Sharon, Sharolette McClanahan, Angie Bates, Nancy Columbia, Carol Green, Debra Guy and Sheila Ward. Back row: teacher Mrs. Asher, John Robert Logan, John Wayne Sartin, William "Cheeseburger" Bush, Denny Nunnelley, Jimmy Roach, Walter Bradley, Gene Ward and Gary Jones. This class was a voluntarily desegregated class in 1958 prior to the mandatory laws passed in 1961. *Courtesy of Libby Sharon Warfield*

Margaret Hall School was in this building on Elm Street in Versailles starting in 1902. The school was founded in 1891. *Courtesy of Fran Allen*

Alpha Gamma Rho fraternity seniors at the University of Kentucky, 1959. Glenn Goebel, Nobel Ruler, is in the back on the left. Others included from back to front: Roger Woeste, Douglas Morgan, Arnold Watson, Harold Grooms, Robert McGibben, Stuart Berryman, Robert Rogers, Glenn Bennett, Hugh Mahan and David Allen. *Courtesy of Arnold Edgar Watson*

Students of the Eastern School of Hair Design, Richmond, being observed by the school's owners, Paul Adams and Jim Barrett. *Courtesy of Mary H. Adams*

Sixth and seventh graders from Margaret Hall School at their Tea Dance, Dec. 7, 1957. *Courtesy of Fran Allen*

Versailles Elementary School band, circa 1958. Front row, left to right: Evelyn Shellenberger, Sharon Lake, Joyce Perkins, unidentified, David Fishback, Ricky Tilghman, Ronald Nabors and unidentified. Second row: (unknown) Foster, unidentified, Mike Maddox, Wanda Cornish, Jack Riley, Barry Brandenburg, Harold Lee and Jennings Edwards. Back row: Danny Dunn, Philip Gaffen, Tommy Benford, unidentified, Wally Howard, unidentified, unidentified and Billy Kincaid.
Courtesy of Harold W. Lee

The fourth-grade class from Clays Mill Elementary walked to the home of one of the students, Patty Sue Jones, for a picnic lunch on a spring day in 1960. The group is in the driveway in front of the carport/patio at the Jones home at 2314 E. Barkley Drive. Patty is third from the right in the back row. Their teacher is Mrs. Fisher. *Courtesy of Miriam Lamy Jones Woolfolk*

University of Kentucky planning committee for construction of the new College of Commerce building, circa 1960. Joe Massie, chairman of the planning committee, is on the left. Third from the left is Dean Cecil Carpenter from the University of Kentucky College of Business and Economics. *Courtesy of Carol Needham Massie*

Advertising for the Spring Festival at St. Leo's Catholic School, Versailles, 1963. St. Leo's Church is in the background. In the back from left to right: Theresa Mangione, Kevin Lane Dearinger, Carol Schoo, Dorothy Ewing and Jay Weisenberger. In front are (unknown) Ward and Tom Fitzgerald. *Courtesy of David Dearinger*

May Day court from Margaret Hall School, Versailles, 1964. *Courtesy of Fran Allen*

Dianne Potter, right, in a dorm room at McGregor Hall at Eastern Kentucky University, circa 1965. *Courtesy of Cynthia L. Hayes*

Third graders at Arlington School, 1966. Their teacher is Mrs. Johnson. *Courtesy of Mary Jo Smith*

Kappa Alpha Theta alumnae at the governor's mansion, April 2, 1965. Gov. Ned Breathitt was the houseboy at the Theta House at the University of Kentucky when most of the women lived there and he was a student at the university. Included are: Gov. Ned Breathitt, Frances Holeman Breathitt, Martha Ann Wilson Haydon, Betty Ann Stoll, Betty Bogess, Pat Chase Corman, Sharon Richards, Julia Ann Hurst Carty, Margaret Tweedy Regan, Joan Kenny Layman, Ann Carson Asbury, Polly Mulkey, Betty Patterson, Grace (unknown), Nancy Brewer Womach, Mary Halmhuber, Nancy Bird, Mary Jo Bishop Jones, Mary Ellen Prace Gant, Virginia Ann Hall and Patti Perrone Thomas. *Courtesy of Pat Chase Corman*

Reunion of the Henry Clay High School class of 1940. First row on the floor, left to right: June Houston Tunstill, Anita Roos Baker, Helynn Gillis Stewart, Bessie Bannon, Thelma Terry Labhart, Lillian Haddix Meeks, Frances Ledford Haggard, Helen Ellsworth Adkins, Helen Truby and Wilma Bowman Sullivan. Second row: David Sinclair (Schwartz), Frances Sammons Perkins, Leland Smith, Bobby Dodd (class of 1942), Troy Strong, J.B. Osborne, Charles Reeves, Josephine Allender Bryant, Vernon "June" Bryant, Lucille Meadors Simmons and Doris Cornette Moore. Third row: Martha Koppius Hall, Helen Kafoglis Anthracopoulos, Mary Curtis Wallace, Caroline Mason Wood, Frances Kelley, Lillian Heaton Markussen, Mabel Gumm McKenney, Mary Elizabeth Baxter Lake, Marietta McRae Rogers, Ilena Jackson Schneiter and Ann Crutcher Sither. Fourth row: Martha Barnes Hendricks, Carl Diamond, Jack Hammond, Bill Tuney, James Gallagher, Adalin Stern Wichman, Martha Palmer Shandrick, Dorothy Gibson Kelley, Barbara Smedley and Peggy Forman Courtney. Fifth row: Jack Pennock, Monroe Shephard, Vernon Wilford, Miller Campbell, Charles Barker, Milton Kafoglis, Robert Pierratt, Don Worthington, Dick Webb and Ramon Cord. *Courtesy of June H. Tunstill*

The girls of Mrs. Chiles' second-grade class at Arlington School, North Limestone, 1965-66. *Courtesy of Mary Jo Smith*

The boys of Mrs. Chiles' second-grade class at Arlington School, North Limestone, 1965-66. *Courtesy of Mary Jo Smith*

Sixth-grade class at Douglass Elementary taught by Virginia French, 1969. *Courtesy of Virginia H. French*

Tates Creek Elementary class, circa 1968. Antoine Smithers is the boy nearest the wall on the back table on the left. *Courtesy of Betty Yates Smithers*

Students at Clays Mill School, Lexington, 1970. Ann Todd Pearce is in the front row on the right. *Courtesy of Julia Pearce*

Yates School students, Lexington, 1969. Mrs. Maley was their teacher. Gail Pearce is in the second row on the left. *Courtesy of Julia Pearce*

Mrs. Head's fifth-grade class, Yates School on New Circle Road, 1968-69. Front row, left to right: Debbie Ragland, Debbie Collins, Tina Hickey, Debbie P. (unknown), Donna Burton and Joyce Reynolds. Second row: Mrs. Head, Wayne Staley, Hobert (unknown), Daryl Brannock, Frank Williams, Keithen Betterman, Mike McGuire and Garnet (unknown). Third row: Beverley Waits, Donald Bates, Mary Jo Oder, Dorenda Reynolds, Becky Smith, R.C. Foster and Tom (unknown). Fourth row: Bobby Owens, David Devine, Kim Mink, Kenny Woolums, Alene Banks, John Curless and Perry Wade. *Courtesy of Mary Jo Smith*

SPORTS & LEISURE

O f all the photos in this book, the images of Central Kentuckians at play in the 1940s, '50s and '60s could be most easily mistaken for photos taken today.

There are groups of boys in short pants, with someone holding a basketball. There are rows of young men in shoulder pads and jerseys, football helmets at their feet.

There is the jockey, riding high on a thoroughbred, ready to run the oval at Keeneland Race Course.

But look closely and you will see the subtle differences. The Keeneland Clubhouse, for example, has undergone numerous changes. Blue Grass Field, now Blue Grass Airport, is barely recognizable. And Joyland Park? Long gone.

Two surprises in this section: Singer and movie star Pat Boone, in town to film "April Love," and a young football coach with movie star looks, Paul "Bear" Bryant.

Keeneland Race Course, 1940. *Courtesy of Transylvania University Library, J. Winston Coleman Jr. Collection*

Martha L. Dickston, Mary Gregory, Florence Boone Stevenson and Mary Boone Dickston, left to right, at Keeneland Race Course, 1942. *Courtesy of Lou and Mary Beth Noel*

Loradale Democrats baseball team, Russell Cave Road, circa 1942. Front row, left to right: Victor Carr, Chester Carr, Tinnie Carr, Douglas Carr, Lee Carr and Wesley Carr. Back row: Robert Carr, Thomas Carr, James Carr Sr., Charles Carr and Spinner Moore. *Courtesy of James and Helen Carr*

African-American girls' swimming class, Joyland pool, June 1944. When instructor Lucian P. Garrett gave tests at the Douglas Pool to see what his pupils had learned during their *Herald-Leader* swim course for girls, these girls took the lead by covering the longer test routes. Swimming the length of the pool (105 feet) were: Nancy Goodloe, Gloria Jean Harris, Gertrude Mitchell, Alma Jackson, Vada Rutherford, Ann Carroll Findley, Dorothy McDowell, Estella Hack, Margaret Arnold and Galatian Miller. Swimming 75 to 80 feet were: Marie Hardin, Mary Carter, Mary Lou Latimaer, Catherine Underwood and Barbar Galewood. Swimming 50 to 55 feet were Earlene Howard and Mercia Cassell. With the girls are instructor Garrett, assistant instructor Leonard Mills Jr. and Mrs. H.H. Rowe, director of Douglas Park and city recreation. *Courtesy of University of Kentucky Libraries 1.13-534.08*

Nicholasville High School football players, circa 1945. Front row, left to right: Benny Gill, Clay Watts and Gene Royse. Second row: Ralph Walker, Billy Cole, (unknown) Tudor, James Belcher, Batie Watts, Dewey Walker, J.B. Knight, Ed Clark, Fred Murphy and Bale Wilson. Third row: Leslie May, Joe Watts, Frank Bishop and James Cooper. Fourth row: Howard Teater, Howard Churchill, (unknown) Lawson and Jack Wilson. Back row: Robert Hager, Tom Bailey and Reb. McGohon. *Courtesy of Jessamine County Historical Society*

Millville Elementary School basketball team, 1948, left to right: Bob Etherington, Cecil Woolums, unidentified, unidentified, John Darsie, Benny Cox, Ira Tupts, unidentified, Doug Sutherland and unidentified. *Courtesy of Lillie Tilghman Cox*

Rosetta Jones and Anna Bell Middleton at Douglas Park, Lexington, circa 1942. *Courtesy of DeMaris M. Duncan*

Lafayette High School football team, first team of the school, fall of 1946. Coach Ishmael, on the far right, later became principal of the school. Jimmy Humphrey is the sixth person standing in the third row. *Courtesy of Jim Humphrey*

Joyland Casino, circa 1947. From left to right: Jack Dearinger, Annie Lane, Bernie Thornton, Jack Barnes, unidentified and Tina Barnes. *Courtesy of Kevin Lane Dearinger*

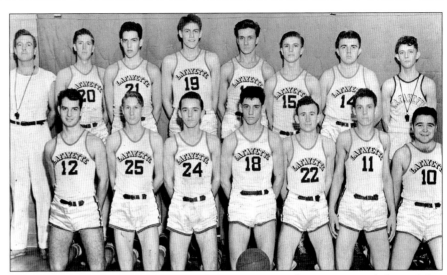

Lafayette High School's first basketball team, 1939-40. Front row, left to right: Jack Ireland, Paul McDaniel, Harold Easley, Jack Clark, James (unknown), Monk Honican and Ted McDaniel. Back row: coach Maurice Jackson, Clyde McDaniel, Troy Adams, Ed Lander, Bill Linkenfelter, (unknown) Daily, Newell Hadden and manager Ike Pennebaker. *Courtesy of Harold and Marjorie Easley*

Mary Jo Chase, front, and Mary Strode rowing on Herrington Lake, circa 1948. Camping on Herrington Lake in the 1940s was a favorite pastime for many Boyle County residents. The swimming pool at the lake also attracted many young people. *Courtesy of Mary Jo Chase Burke*

Everett McCann on a horse at the Keeneland Race Course, circa 1950. *Courtesy of DeMaris M. Duncan*

Crowd at Blue Grass Field awaiting the return of the victorious Wildcats who had beaten Mississippi 47-0, October 1949. *Courtesy of University of Kentucky Librariess* *1.04-1350.01*

Keeneland Race Course, spring of 1946. *Courtesy of University of Kentucky Libraries* *2.03-4.06*

University of Kentucky coaching staff, spring 1946. From left to right: head coach Paul "Bear" Bryant, Frank Moseley and Carney Leslie, all products of Alabama football; Mike Balitsaris, former Tennessee end, and Joe Atkinson, former captian and guard at Vanderbilt. *Courtesy of University of Kentucky Libraries* *1.13-431*

Grace Baptist Church fast-pitch softball, 1953. Front row, left to right: George "Fritz" Ritchey, Kelly Chowning, Roy Flynn, Louis Fox, Herbert Cox, H.K. Reams and unidentified. Back row: Jimmy Littrel, Ralph Shields, Doug Hager, Frank Bennett, Jack Baker, Earl Gipson, Buster True, Paul Brown, Elmo Grimes and Milton "Bunnie" Taylor. The batboy is David Fox. *Courtesy of Pat Ritchey*

Great Crossing High School basketball players, 1952. Front row, left to right: Roy Carr, Johnny Ginn and Herman Carr. Back row: Bobby Carr, Rhodes Carr, Jimmy Carr and Logan Carr. All were brothers except Ginn, who was a cousin. *Courtesy of James and Helen Carr*

Swimming in South Elkhorn Creek, Fort Springs, Lexington, circa 1950. In front, left to right: Harold Granville, John Robert Byrd, Earlene Wright, Marian Gilmore and Thurman Wright. In the back are Roy Taylor Jr. and Ray Granville. *Courtesy of DeMaris M. Duncan*

Carlisle Musketeers, "The Coachless Wonders," 1954. They played the first three games of the season without a coach, winning each game. They were lead through those games by Ben Henry Pumphrey. *Courtesy of Don J. Dampier*

Miss Barbara Harper, mounted on Miss Inquisitive, and Miss Priscilla Roberts at Keeneland Race Course, June 1956. The young women were training for the Junior League horse show. *Courtesy of Barbara Harper Bach*

Mike Walker and Rosemary Cox at Joyland Park on July 13, 1952. *Courtesy of Rosemary C. Johnson*

April Love, starring Pat Boone, left, being made in Lexington, June 1957. *Courtesy of University of Kentucky Libraries 1.12-1678.01*

Kob Ryans' Riding Academy on Parker's Mill Road, 1959. Barbara Harper, one of the riding instructors, is on the right, with Marta Kauffman on the left. *Courtesy of Barbara Harper Bach*

Fraternal Order of Police youth basketball team, 1959-60. Donald Chumley was the team's coach. *Courtesy of Donald Chumley*

State championship football team from Versailles High School, 1962. *Courtesy of Woodford County Historical Society*

Herald-Leader Free Learn-to-Swim course at Joyland Park, July 1961. *Courtesy of University of Kentucky Libraries S.1645*

Theocracy with jockey Luther Adkins after winning the Kentucky Thoroughbred Breeders Association Purse at Miles Park, July 12, 1961. On the left are Paul Adams, owner, and Robert Steele, trainer. *Courtesy of Mary H. Adams*

Red Cross life saving class at Woodamere Pool, Versailles, circa 1962. *Courtesy of Fran Allen*

Sadieville basketball team, April 17, 1963. *Courtesy of Georgetown and Scott County Historical Society*

Cubs Little League team from Jessamine County, 1968. Front row, left to right: Jesse Jackson, Butch Bogie, unidentified, unidentified, Jesse Lemay, unidentified and Lloyd Watkins. Middle row: Ronnie Bruner, Morris Wayne, (unknown) Settle, unidentified, Mike Briener, Jervis Hitch, Jesse Baker, Glen Teater and Ronnie Hammond. Back row: Howard Teater, Gene Henkle and Gene Royse. *Courtesy of Howard C. Teater*

Horse named Huck Finn trained and driven by Gibson White at the Red Mile racetrack, Sept. 26, 1964. Presenting the trophy for the fourth race is Barbara Harper Bach, outrider at the racetrack. Holding the horse is owner Alan Brewer, renowned local equine artist. Gibson White is the subject of the book "Born to Trot," written by Marguerite Henry. *Courtesy of Barbara Harper Bach*

Field hockey at Margaret Hall School, 1968. *Courtesy of Fran Allen*

COMMUNITY & SOCIETY

More than any other section, this is the snapshot part of this book. Captured for all time is a family with a snowman, children in front of a Christmas tree, some people sitting on the fender of a car, back when cars had fenders.

Here you have the Dearinger children, the Yates family, the Mayfield twins. There is a child's visit with Santa (who hasn't changed a bit over the years), railroad men in front of an engine and daring boys on a backyard campout.

There is, no doubt, a story behind every photo here.

You probably have photos like these in an album in the back of a closet somewhere. If you or no one you know is in these photos, looking through them might inspire you to pull out your own stories.

Opening night of *Home is the Hunter* in Harrodsburg, 1963. From left to right: Boonie Noel; Charlie Noel, secretary of the board of directors of the production and Bud Dedman, owner of Beaumont Inn and president of the board of directors of the production. *Courtesy of Lou and Mary Beth Noel*

Marion Miley boarding a plane after winning the Kentucky women's state championship at Audubon Country Club in Louisville in 1940. *Courtesy of Lexington History Museum*

Humphrey family front yard of 114 Hamilton Park, 1940. From left to right: Carl Liberman, Harvey Liberman, James Humphrey, Billy Humphrey and Jimmie Humphrey. *Courtesy of Jim Humphrey*

Raymond Cox and Edith Patricia Brown with a 1931 Chevrolet at the first home of Raymond and Evelyn Cox on the Mike Faust farm, circa 1940. *Courtesy of Rosemary C. Johnson*

The Wash family on their farm in Woodford County, 1945. On the left in the tractor seat is Robert Wash with his son, Wendell. The boy with his hand on the wheel is Gary Chism. In front, Allen and Mildred Wash are holding Brenda Campbell and Linda Wash. Sitting on the tractor hood is John Wash holding Mona Campbell. *Courtesy of Brenda C. Poole*

James Carr Sr. family, Scott County: James, Anna Mae, Waunita, Josephine, Bonnie, Lorraine and Doug. *Courtesy of James and Helen Carr*

Wallace Tilghman with his truck at home in Versailles, 1942. *Courtesy of Lillie Tilghman Cox*

Coleman Morton gathering coal for heating water to scald hogs in Uttinger Town, Lexington, circa 1945. *Courtesy of DeMaris M. Duncan*

Everett McCann, left, on hog-killing day in Uttinger Town, Lexington, circa 1945. *Courtesy of DeMaris M. Duncan*

Tom Thumb wedding at Kenwick School, Henry Clay Boulevard, Lexington, circa 1940. *Courtesy of Frank and Joy Fugazzi*

Playing croquet in the front yard at 114 Hamilton Park, circa 1945. Left to right: Jimmie Humphrey, Tommy Gray, Don Cooper and Billy Humphrey. *Courtesy of Jim Humphrey*

Lucy Logan Massie with her first grandchild, Spivey Massie, daughter of Dr. and Mrs. W.K. Massie. *Courtesy of Carol Needham Massie*

Noah and Lena Griffith in their tobacco field in Spears, circa 1946. *Courtesy of Gwendolyn Griffith Powell*

June Tunstill, Katherine Cramer and Niana Jackson, 1944. The young women, who all worked at the Department of Agriculture, sang as a trio during that time. June sent this picture to her husband, Jay Tunstill, who was serving in Trinidad, British West Indies, during World War II. Niana wrote the Henry Clay High School song, "Get Going, Blue Devils," which was used from that time forward. *Courtesy of June H. Tunstill*

Gwendolyn Griffith in front of her father's truck, circa 1946. Not all the farmers had a truck at that time, so Mr. Griffith contracted frequently to haul things, like livestock, hay and crops, for other farmers. *Courtesy of Gwendolyn Griffith Powell*

Betty Reynolds and John P. Boyd on the grounds of the University of Kentucky, 1943. John was from Pennsylvania and was stationed at the university in the Army Specialized Training Program. The couple later married and remained in Lexington. *Courtesy of Betty Boyd*

Margie Cropper on the steps of Morrison Hall on the Transylvania College campus, circa 1944. *Courtesy of Harold and Marjorie Easley*

Family on the Setliff Peel farm on Sugar Creek Pike in Jessamine County, 1942. From left to right: Gladys Peel, Leona Reynolds, Roberta Roberts, Elizabeth Jasper holding Elizabeth Ann and Betty Boyd. *Courtesy of Betty Boyd*

Boonesboro Beach, 1945. Left to right: Ann Sharon Richardson; Annie Lane; Bernie Thornton and Bernie's brother, George Thornton. *Courtesy of Kevin Lane Dearinger*

Clayton Richardson, Woodford County, circa 1945. He was a lineman for Kentucky Utilities and long-time fireman for both Versailles and Woodford County fire departments. *Courtesy of Harold W. Lee*

Carolyn Sue Tilghman with her bicycle, Versailles, circa 1948. *Courtesy of Lillie Tilghman Cox*

Matilda Young with her granddaughter, Lillie Tilghman, on the Case tractor on their farm off Mason Headley Road in Lexington, circa 1945. Lillie B Young is peeping over the wheel. *Courtesy of Lillie Tilghman Cox*

Anna L. Lane, age 19, in Castlewood Park, 1945. *Courtesy of Kevin Lane Dearinger*

Sisters Iva Jean, left, and Gladys Barnes, circa 1944. *Courtesy of Gwendolyn Griffith Powell*

Boys clinging to the top and sides of the YMCA billboard to see Bess, the "horse with the human mind," on the courthouse lawn, September 1946. *Courtesy of University of Kentucky Libraries 1.01-239.021*

C&O railroad employees at the Netherland yards, Lexington, circa 1948. Left to right: Alex Eldridge (yard foremen), E.B. McQuown (telegrapher) and Jimmy Sullivan (switchman). *Courtesy of Marion Eldridge*

Jessie Reynolds in front of Reynolds Grocery on Virginia Avenue, 1949. She and her husband, A.B. Reynolds, owned the store. *Courtesy of Betty Boyd*

Barry Dickston, age 6, the youngest member of Millersberg Military Institute, 1943. *Courtesy of Barry Dickston*

Lillie Tilghman, left, with friend Betty Million in their piano recital gowns, made by Lillie's mother, Alice Tilghman, 1947. Betty died of cancer during her senior year of high school. *Courtesy of Lillie Tilghman Cox*

Wallace C. Yates with his two dates, Mary Chenault on the left and Liz Cowherd on the right, at the 1948 Senior Prom at Dunbar High School, 1948. *Courtesy of Betty Yates Smithers*

Paul Adams, "Mr., Paul," of the B.B. Smith Beauty Salon, won the area hair styling contest sponsored by the Lexington Unit, National Hairdressers and Cosmetologists Association, Nov. 16, 1955. The model displays the hairstyle that took top honors. Mr. Paul later owned the Stylette and Fashion Flair Salon on Romany Road. He and Jim Barrett also owned and operated the Eastern School of Hair Design in Richmond. In the early 1960s, the Stylette Salon charged $1.75 for a shampoo and set and $12.50 for a permanent wave. *Courtesy of Mary H. Adams*

Siblings Joann Richardson, Mary Margaret Richardson and Paul D. Richardson holding his nephew, Harold W. Lee, Versailles, circa 1949. *Courtesy of Harold W. Lee*

Noah Griffith Jr. and Sr. on their home farm in Spears, 1951. *Courtesy of Gwendolyn Griffith Powell*

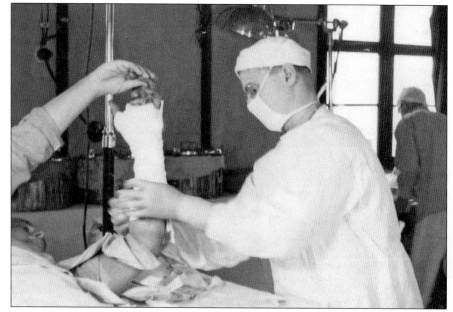

Dr. William Kenney Massie, orthopedic surgeon and inventor of the "Massie Nail," the first means of flexibility after hip surgery. *Courtesy of Carol Needham Massie*

Snow White and the Seven Dwarfs in Santa's Christmas Caravan, December 1955. The group went to Eastern State Hospital, Juluis Marks Sanitorium, Colored Orphans Home and U.S. Public Health Hospital as a part of Jaycees Community Christmas Program sponsored by Fayette County Playground & Recreation Board. Starting at the rear left: Pat Ritchey, unidentified, Janet (unknown), Peggy Scott and unidentified. Front: unidentified, Phillip (unknown) and David (unknown). Snow White, who got the part by raising the most funds, is unidentified. *Courtesy of Pat Ritchey*

Louis Shimfessel with his sons, Richard, left, and John, 1950. They lived at Moss Acres Farm, Fayette County. *Courtesy of Andrea Hobbs*

Sledding at the home of Joe and Chris Massie, 425 W. 7th St., Lexington, January 1951. From left to right: Spivey Massie, Anne Randall Short, Billy Massie, Kenney Massie, Carol Massie and Lucy Massie. *Courtesy of Carol Needham Massie*

Gathered in the home of Anna Lee and Henry Devers, circa 1953, in the front row, left to right: Karen Sue, Floyd Allen and Linda Jo Devers. In back are Evelyn and Anna Lee Devers. *Courtesy of Linda Jo Bell*

Jack and Gwendolyn Carroll, Dec. 25, 1949, on their first wedding anniversary. *Courtesy of Gwendolyn Griffith Powell*

Barbara Harper with her sister, Mary Jane, and brother, William "Bucky" Harper Jr., on Christmas morning, 1954. *Courtesy of Barbara Harper Bach*

Coleman Morton, Lexington, circa 1950. *Courtesy of DeMaris M. Duncan*

DeMaris McCann in her Easter suit made by her Aunt Rosetta Jones, Uttinger Town, Lexington, circa 1950. *Courtesy of DeMaris M. Duncan*

Birthday party for A.B. Reynolds at Lock 8 of the Kentucky River, 1953. It turned out to be his last birthday. He is pictured with one son and many of his grandchildren. *Courtesy of Betty Boyd*

Pat Ritchey on Billy the horse, 1952. *Courtesy of Pat Ritchey*

Paula and Sandra Mayfield, twin daughters of Raymond and Mary Ella Smithers, Mayfield, 1952. *Courtesy of Betty Yates Smithers*

Jack White on one of the family farm work horses, 1952. Jack and his brothers would ride the workhorses to the creek for a drink during the break for lunch. *Courtesy of Jack A. White*

Edna Grace Davis and her son, Dickie, on the fender of their car at Lock 8 of the Kentucky River, 1953. *Courtesy of Betty Boyd*

Million-dollar fire at the R.J. Reynolds tobacco storage warehouse, February 1952. Firemen are silhouetted against burning Warehouse No. 8 on Versailles Road near Angliana Avenue. *Courtesy of University of Kentucky Libraries 1.07-471.04*

Group of Lexington area youngsters with their hula hoops, September 1958. *Courtesy of University of Kentucky Libraries 1.14-2192.02*

Pam, David and Kevin Dearinger at 298 Douglas Ave., Versailles, on a warm Christmas Day, 1954. *Courtesy of Kevin Lane Dearinger*

Patricia Ann Kelley, April 1956. *Courtesy of Arnold Edgar Watson*

Twins Jacquline Yvonne and Gwendolyn Marie French, daughters of William and Virginia French, 1955. *Courtesy of Virginia H. French*

Lydia Harris's hand-hooked rug won first prize out of 160 entries at a craft fair sponsored by the Lexington Division of Parks and Recreation, Sept. 1, 1955. *Courtesy of Beverley H. McDonald*

The Yates family, 1955. In front are Charlene and Charles. Middle row, left to right: Ann, Annabelle, William and Betty. Standing in back: Dorothy, Robert, William and Mattie. *Courtesy of Betty Yates Smithers*

Alvin and Calvin Mayfield, twin sons of Raymond and Mary Ella Smithers Mayfield, 1954. *Courtesy of Betty Yates Smithers*

Wedding party of Lillian Burdett and Alger Howard, Aug. 31, 1952. From left to right: Mary Shelton, Dorothy Coleman, bride and groom, Theodore Jackson, William Burdett, Dorothy Call and Virginia French. Flower girls are Mary and Audrey Coleman. *Courtesy of Virginia H. French*

Jock Conley and Judy Shrout ready for the Carlisle prom, 1955. They are in the living room of Jock's good friend, Don Dampier. *Courtesy of Don J. Dampier*

Libby Sharon's third birthday party in the family's back yard on Winter Street, Midway, June 1, 1955. From left to right: Libby, Sandy Clifton, Karen Clifton and Peggy Sharon. *Courtesy of Libby Sharon Warfield*

Purcell's Department Store Santa holding Pam Ritchey with her sister, Pat, 1956. *Courtesy of Pat Ritchey*

Birthday girls Sally Jo Jones, left, and Leslie Busch, October 1958. *Courtesy of Miriam Lamy Jones Woolfolk*

Don and Jim Gash and friends camp out overnight in the back yard of the Gash home on East Barkley Drive, summer of 1957. *Courtesy of Miriam Lamy Jones Woolfolk*

Dinner at The Renfrew House, circa 1960. Seated around the table, from left to right: Frances Wickliffe, Bill Cole, Betty Cummings, Louis Greenberg, Pete Wickliffe, Boonie Noel and Shirley Greenberg. Earl Cummings and an unidentified woman are standing behind. *Courtesy of Lou and Mary Beth Noel*

Earl and June Willoughby on their wedding day, June 3, 1955. They were married at Versailles Baptist Church. *Courtesy of June and Earl Willoughby*

Carol Massie, sophomore attendant to Miss Henry Clay Homecoming, November 1958. *Courtesy of Carol Needham Massie*

Littrell family reunion at Castlewood Park near the old barn, 1959. From left to right: Frankie Oder, Georgia Jo House, Ernestine Tennie Otis, Aretta Bobo, Margaret Hamm, Mary Williams, Chester Littrell and Gilbert Littrell. *Courtesy of Mary Jo Smith*

Dedication of the amphitheater in Harrodsburg, 1963. The speaker is Robert Emmett McDowell, playwright of *Home is the Hunter*. Local businessmen formed a committee to bring the amphitheater and outdoor drama to Harrodsburg. Front row, left to right: Joe Russell, Don Billy Robinson, Mrs. Robert McDowell, unidentified in the back, Rev. John Akers, Boonie Noel behind the podium, Ola Frances Royalty, Cassie Lee, Gene Royalty, unidentified, Jason Bugg, unidentified and Mrs. Jason Bugg. *Courtesy of Lou and Mary Beth Noel*

Patricia Ann Kelley and Arnold E. Watson in Winchester, Easter 1959. *Courtesy of Arnold Edgar Watson*

Fire at Palmer's in West Side Plaza on Georgetown Street, circa 1960. *Courtesy of Donald Chumley*

Bobby Burnton driving his buggy on Main Street in Nicholasville, 1960. The horse's name is Ajax. *Courtesy of Howard C. Teater*

Workmen tearing down the Opera House theater, one of Lexington's old landmarks at 143 N. Broadway, August 1961. *Courtesy of University of Kentucky Libraries S.2040*

Retirement gathering for Chief Clerk D.J. Mahannes with the L & N Railroad, July 30, 1960. Front row, left to right: Marion Eldridge, Harry Scully, Mrs. Gerald Walker, Mrs. D.J. Mahannes, Ms. Thelma Norton and Mrs. Benning. Back row: Paul Walters, Gerald Walker, J.M. Johnston, D.J. Mahannes, Paul McDaniel, Ray Pollitte, Robert Harris and Mr. Benning. *Courtesy of Marion Eldridge*

Christmas 1961 at the Smithers home at 370 E. 2nd St. Left to right: Thomas Jr., Debra holding Antoine, Michael and Calvin. *Courtesy of Betty Yates Smithers*

University of Kentucky student Jim Embry as he waited in front of Memorial Coliseum to hear George Wallace speak during his presidential campaign, 1968. *Courtesy of Jim Embry*

Susan Ball Alexander, Maple Hill Farm, with her companion of more than 25 years, Lillie B Young, at the dedication of the new Woodford Memorial Hospital, circa 1965. *Courtesy of Lillie Tilghman Cox*

Lexington residents Ann, Dianne and Preston Potter in front of Alumni Coliseum at Eastern Kentucky University, May 1966. *Courtesy of Cynthia L. Hayes*

Linda Jo and Freddy Wynn, front, and Shirley Wynn and Floyd Allen at the home of Lula Bell Wynn, Frankfort Pike, Georgetown, circa 1961. *Courtesy of Linda Jo Bell*

Kelley L. Watson, age two, helping her mom wash the dishes, 1964. *Courtesy of Arnold Edgar Watson*

Baptism day of Andrea Shimfessel, summer of 1967. From left to right: Robert Bunting, Ethel Alexander, Betty Bunting holding Andrea and Louise Stivers. *Courtesy of Andrea Hobbs*

TV and film star Desi Arnaz appears with his wife, Edith Mack Hirsh, during the Keeneland Horse Sale of Breeding Stock, November 1963. The Arnaz group from Corona, Calif., included farm manager Charles Zoeller. *Courtesy of University of Kentucky Libraries U.2840*

Junior Girl Scout troop on Airdrie Farm learning how to light a fire, 1967. They finally gave up and used matches. The girl on the far left is Cindy Sharon. The two girls on the right are Mary Starks and Mary Ellen Pittman. *Courtesy of Libby Sharon Warfield*

William French III, left, and Karl French on the front step of their home at 423 N. Upper St., 1969. *Courtesy of Virginia H. French*

Franklin Heath Leigh with his son, Franklin Wesley, on Ashmore Avenue, Versailles, 1969. *Courtesy of Joann Leigh*